LEADERSHIP: A LONG STORY SHORT

www.iamronholloway.com

ISBN-10: 0692192972
ISBN-13: 978-0692192979

Edited by Mark Ingutti

Dedicated to every boss, coworker, shipmate, coach, and teammate I ever had. You all taught me something–good, bad, or ugly.

Oh, and thanks, College Park.

Love you, Sis

Love you, Lil Foots

"You want to be a great leader? Listen. If you want to be a great leader, you only have to remember one thing: It's *all* about your people. It ain't about *you* no more. It ain't about *your* awards or *your* recognition; it's about *them*. Because they write your resume; they write your evaluations; they will ultimately decide whether you're successful or not."

BMC Gene Peters, USS Nassau (LHA-4)

LEADERSHIP ➡

← A LONG STORY SHORT

⬆ BY RON HOLLOWAY

CONTENTS

INTRODUCTION i

WHY ARE YOU HERE 1

THE EMOTIONALLY INTELLIGENT LEADER 5

ENGAGING THE DISENGAGED 33

YOU GOT SKILLS 59

QUOTES 73

OPEN LETTER 77

LEADERSHIP KEY TERMS 81

INTRODUCTION

People are different. What was done to me created me. I'm sure the same holds true for you, whether or not you consciously recognize it. Based on that, we all create (fill in the blank) narratives based on what we believe is important. Ergo, we see what we want to see. Every leader may be different, but the basic elements of leadership do not change. As you'll see going forward, throughout our lives we hope our experiences become synonymous with wisdom. For example, we learn concepts like "greatness needs adversity"; however, most times we're blissfully unaware of cause and effect.

This book is about the method of sensible, user-friendly leadership. I wrote *Leadership: A Long Story Short* because I don't want you or anyone else to grasp leadership with a mob mentality. By that I mean leadership is a long story short, but it isn't binary logic–this or that, right or wrong, Android or iPhone. That last one, though. Yes, nuance does exist; it's just not overly complicated. As you read, you'll see nuance. You'll see the focus is a warm Snuggie® converging on sensibilities through knowledge and understanding–all of which are inspired from the hardtop basketball court to steel-plated decks.

We people are always concerned about

our leaderships abilities. We secretly crave discernment. Why? Because leadership aptitude transcends parenting, relationships, team sports, and our 9-to-5s. Whether in business, government, or the family, people reach most decisions through some form of leadership. Therefore, during our time together, you'll see discernment on text. Consider this book a text message with punctuation or an email, if you know what that is. (I'm told it's still a thing apparently. Who knew?) Anyway, and now that I have your money, I can tell you that the greatest gifts you'll receive during this reading is the vision and fundamental resources necessary to lead. I'm going to give you both, because a vision without resources is just an illusion or hallucination.

Like it or not, you're a leader–or you will be. Take a deep breath. Keep calm and read on. Learn, as I did, why it's all about people. Learn where the power lies. Learn your primary objective. One objective? Uh huh. As a leader, you have ONE goal for your organization, family, team, etc.: to get better.

And it's every day, every game, every Reveille, every possession.

Keep hope alive. Please enjoy.

WHY ARE YOU HERE?

At least he's still breathing.

His rapid breaths slowed as all realisms of being alive were re-established. I know because he burped and his snot ran down unnoticed over the top, then bottom, lip. The secret was that he hated being told what to do. He hated the process, which meant revealing in an accomplishment that revealed all his fears. Easily his phobia was the uncomforting. The nervous gesture of eyes staring down and/or away eschewed these secrets to success, which starred right back as resilience in tough times and seeing challenges as opportunities.

Let me ask you something

Why do you want to be a leader? Again, *why* do *you* want to be a leader? Is it self-interest? What do you hope to gain? Perhaps it's fame or validation. Leadership isn't about canonization. Maybe you're looking for love. Some of you are probably checking a dating app right now, swiping right when you should have swiped left. Anyway, those things may be what you want, but that's not why you are ultimately labeled a leader.

Back in the day, Lincoln and MLK had a "why" and knew a "why." More recently, we would say the same of Steve Jobs, Sean Carter, and Jeff Bezos. You see, in these cases the "why" was vision and belief. The "why" was promotion, strength and growth, and the "why" was a beautiful tango of value and community. Also, Lincoln's and King's intent on engagement meant the "why" started with and was within them. Now that you know, ask yourself: Right now, am I engaged? Am I getting my absolute best? Not the best girlfriend or boyfriend– the best, you silly.

Stay focused, people…

Are you moving forward in terms of your vision, relationships, and service? Are you collaborating with others? Are you curating those relationships and therefore reaching your max output because 1) you are sensitive to difference, and 2) you better understand your community of values, attitudes, and beliefs? These questions are important because *perspective informs decision-making.* Questions. Questions. Questions. No, you are not on Jeopardy. So far, you are probably thinking, "This is a game of '21 Questions'"; however, unlike Rube Goldberg, this machine is an exercise in making leadership–what some assume complex– simple.

Here is a heartbreaking example of why those questions in the paragraphs above are important.

I grew up loving the NBA. I am a Milwaukee Bucks fan first but was also an avid Los Angeles Lakers fan. In fact, growing up, Lakers star Earvin "Magic" Johnson was my favorite NBA player. So, it hurt me to my core when in 2004 the LA Lakers had arguably the *greatest* team ever assembled but lost in the NBA Championship finals to the Detroit Pistons, a team that many felt were far inferior. But Detroit had what many believed the Lakers did not: leadership, engagement, and alliance. Detroit could answer all those questions above and understood the "why" for each, whereas the Lakers could not, which resulted in a loss of maximum potential, an NBA Championship, and me crying myself to sleep over not one but two Nacho Bell Grandes. Super-duper paid for that the next morning–poo emoji.

Let's get back to being serious. Great leaders throughout history have always understood the importance of "why" as it relates to leading people and accomplishing goals; this is true of presidents explaining why you should vote for them or why bartenders give you excellent service because you tip the best. Don't believe me? Listen to any great fictional or non-fictional battle commanders (or coach) as they speak to their troops prior to battle. I guarantee you their call to victory is laced and dripping with "why." The point here is this: Good leadership is sweat equity, both mentally and physically; you get what you give. And what you get is return on investment. Leaders think forward. Leaders understand the importance of new beginnings, new motivations, new "whys." Progress is the "why." Leaders like you are the "why." Great leaders understand it is not a matter of "Will I be a participator? Or will I be an observer?" Leaders understand it is a combination of both.

For example, please take a moment to answer the following questions about leaders you may know:

How do you know they are good leaders?
What traits and behaviors do they share?
Does effectiveness play a part in you labeling them leaders?
Are they able to influence the environment?

Now ask yourself *why* you answered the questions the way you did.

I'll tell you why (pun intended.) Because the "why" is the common denominator of every question you just answered. This is why they are good leaders. Why are those traits and behaviors important to you? Why are they effective? Why is effectiveness an important determination? Why are they able to influence?

I'm harping. I know. I just want you to understand that experiences, social awareness, and, more importantly, self-reflection are important aspects of great leadership.

THE EMOTIONALLY INTELLIGENT LEADER

As I watched, with each trial and participation confusion confounded his face, I heard him rehashing missed information and practical limits. "Will I ever be able to do this?" he asked himself. "Maybe I'm weak. And who else knows it?" Water dripping off him ubiquitously, one could see he tried to be a superstar—holding everything close to the chest. In short, he was pushed albeit internally or externally to engage and reengage. How could he not, as he accurately measured the performance of others (as well as his own).

Aren't we all the same

I cannot exactly pinpoint when, but one late afternoon, I was watching ESPN's Pardon the Interruption with hosts Tony Kornheiser (TK) and Michael Wilbon. During one segment, Wilbon turns toward TK and says a philosopher's quote: "Storytelling is told through a certain prism, and everything that you are impacts the way you tell that story." It had to be one of the most powerful quotes I had ever heard. They were the perfect words and perfect articulation of how I have always wanted to express myself. They were the perfect words and perfect articulation of how I want to be understood. Imagine being a voice trapped in a glass room. Imagine that trapped voice in the glass room looking out into the world. Imagine wanting to share with the souls of others but being reciprocally, environmentally, and socially mute and deaf.

I know. I know. I'm dramatizing a bit.

Yet, as a leader or follower, you may find my hyperbole feels very intimate at times. And, yes, followers are just as important to this short story. Because a leader without followers is just a guy (or gal) going for a walk, as someone once said. As the chapters progress, you'll see more and more that leadership is interpersonal, which leads to one thing I've learned: Leaders must appreciate followers' needs as it relates to values. Webster's defines values as "something such as a principle or quality." On balance, values shape attitudes and behaviors; they forge the prism through which we tell and receive the story. For followers' purposes, having that knowledge available merits dynamic consideration. Good leaders understand that being cognizant of individuals' value systems can be leveraged at all times and at all levels. Why? Because the measure for conceptualizing and appreciating cultural, individual, value-based, and personal motivations has schizophrenic gulfs.

Let me tell you why all this fancy wording and fluff is important. News flash: I'm black. I'm also urban, "woke," and have always been in tune with pop culture. In this regard, I never felt out of place until I joined the Navy (sailors meet all types of people). With that said, early in my enlistment, I had a shipmate who I felt was more black, urban, and pop culture than I was. It, and he, made me question my own blackness. Did I mentioned his ethnicity hailed from an Arabic country? His physical image probably fits any stereotype you just concluded in your mind. We would sit in the ship's lounge, surrounded by dudes in steel-toe boots and exhausted faces, the smell of sweaty skin, the sight of haze gray walls, and televisions blaring sports, while arguing sports, fashion, and politics of the day. You can be sure at any given time someone was eating Flaming Hot Cheetos.

Yet, what makes this so remarkable is that, no matter how much I thought my Arabic friend was exactly like me, his core values appeared much different (and perhaps stronger in certain areas) from mine. At the time, my primary core values focused on teamwork, fairness, competence, and accountability. His core values, on the other hand, focused on spirituality, family, and loyalty. Now, this is not to say he was not a hard worker or lacked any of my aforementioned values, nor I any of his. No, you see, my shipmate was Muslim. Therefore, he needed time and space to leverage his prayer mat, so he could pray five times a day. But wait. We worked sixteen-hour days regularly with non-stop action at times. Did this mean he required a break? Why give him a break in the action? Was his religion any better than mine? Couldn't he make an exception? What about my devotion to accountability and effectiveness? Each of our core values is important in this instance, right? Core values are the reasons for this moral dilemma and ethical challenge. An ethical issue can happen when religious-based demands of one-person conflict with the religious beliefs or basic rights of another.

But as a leader, my focus was ultimately aimed at getting the best outcomes for all involved.

I'd later come to understand my logic as Systems Theory. Dr. Russell Ackoff, an American organizational theorist, concluded the most important aspect of Systems Thinking is examining how the parts interact with one another, not suffering from availability heuristic. If my contemporaries or I had been more concerned with scrutinizing our efforts in relation to the benefit of the sum, then our efficiency would have, no doubt, decreased. Getting the best net-net outcome superseded everything. My ability to be emphatic and allow him the time he needed improved our relationship, team dynamics, and my (probably his too) social development.

Had I focused solely on the mission, my mission, and not respected his wishes, our relationship may have seriously deteriorated, which ultimately would have hurt the primary mission. Here's a secret: By allotting him the time he needed, I got SO much more productivity out of him. Ultimately, he knew I saw him for more than just a nametag. Colleagues and subordinates too saw this modeling of empathy and sensitivity difference. They saw the sensitivity to his story. The important leadership lessons above are this: I was practicing social awareness (we'll dive more into that later), aligning my values with my behavior, creating a trustful atmosphere, and providing the best outcome for stakeholders.

Okay...slow clap...and you can wipe away the tears now. Herein, remember that leaders win when they are clear about what others' core values are. Don't you want to win? In the immortal words of Ricky Bobby, "If you ain't first, you're last." Seriously though, leaders win when they embrace disagreements and encourage individuals to voice their perspectives while acknowledging other point of views; therefore, they continue to grow by being dynamic. Side note: Literally nothing is worse than a static leader. In the end, your primary job is not winning. Your primary job is growth–otherwise known as getting better.

So, the fix is easy then

I could always understand the inspiring spirit rather than the political brain.

- Hannibal (not sure if this was Hannibal,

the Carthaginian General, or Mr. Fava Beans and Chianti)

Any who, I don't understand politics. As Eleanor Roosevelt once said, "I know nothing of politics." For me, politics resembles a dam with cracks and holes. Herein, your energy and power is entirely devoted to clogging the leaks–or the dam blows. Perhaps it starts with one leak. You've patched that crack. Now you noticed another, so you must tend to it. But wait. Then you've noticed a crack somewhere else in the dam; this one is gushing more water than the last, so now you must switch focus because this leak has a lot of "power behind it." Therefore, this particular leak decides where you must focus your power. But guess what. Remember that first leak? Sorry, it's time to grab the gear and resources to "fix the fix." I'm exhausted just writing about said revolutions in maintenance. For a moment, I felt like I was back on a ship or running basketball drills up and down three-story dirt hills in Estherville, Iowa.

Yet, all this talk of cracks and holes and dams and resources and where attention should be paid is an analogy to my next point: emotional intelligence. **Emotional Intelligence**, as a psychological theory, was developed by Peter Salovey and John Mayer. *Psychology Today* defines emotional intelligence as "the ability to identify and manage your own emotions and the emotions of others." As star point guard and sailor, I had been practicing this surreptitiously and ubiquitously without knowing there was a name for it, which I'll explain briefly. Also, speaking of revolutions, emotional intelligence is a revolution in critical thinking–analyzing and deducing before acting, weighing benefits versus the risks, seeing the big picture.

Have a moment with me. Please close your eyes for a second and read along.

Listen big dummy… no one has EVER closed his or her eyes and read along. Nope. Yet to happen.

Unless you're blind. And in that case, I apologize. But if you're blind then you're probably not reading this because it's not in braille. So, then, I really didn't need to apologize in the first place.

Where was I? Are your eyes open? Good. Imagine yourself attending a seminar at a large conference. The conference room is filled with 30 or so random people with whom you have no relations. You are seated and eagerly anticipating the presentation. The seminar speaker grabs the microphone and asks everyone in attendance to count off in fours. Ones with ones. Twos with twos. Threes with threes. Fours with fours. The presenter now tells you to pair up. Ones with threes. Twos with fours. Now that everyone in the room is paired, the speaker says: "Get ready to hold your partner's hands. We're going to do a little dance I created." The speaker waits a minute, looks around the room holding his or her stare, then puts the mic back up to his or her mouth and says, "Sike! That's what we're *not* going to be doing!" The speaker laughs while also instructing participants to take their seats.

Wow, right? Can you imagine your initial emotional reaction? In the words of singer and songwriter D'Angelo, "How does it feel?" If you truly envisioned yourself in the room, maybe you feel that emotion right now. Imagine how the others in the room may feel, especially in the moment when they are instructed to hold hands to do a little dance. More importantly, please think about why you or others may have the emotional reaction. There's that word "why" again. However, can you see how the speaker was able to manipulate your emotions? I'm quite sure you and the other participants would have demonstrated what researchers coin as the *four basic emotions*: anger, sadness, happiness, and fear. You can bet some people would've been so upset that they would be ready to walk out. You can bet some were super fearful. "Dancing! Holding hands! Are you kidding me?" Some of the folks in the session would've been completely agonized, feeling at the end of their ropes. Others, however few, would've been ecstatic and overjoyed. "Turn up! Best workshop ever!"

In the example, the speaker was able to manipulate your emotions. What if you could manipulate your own emotions? Especially, what if you could, with your manner of interaction with others? Listen, I know "manipulate" sounds like a dirty word, but let's redefine and substitute "emotional intelligence." Again, take a concerted, cognitive approach to managing your emotions, expressing yourself, and doing such in a manner that reflects empathy when socializing and building relationships.

Think about how you deal with stress, stressful relationships, and interactions. Think about the emotions that ensue. You can do better, right? Of course, you can do better. I sure know I can. By appreciating and managing your emotions, you can reduce problems and stress and improve productivity and relationships.

Moving right along.

How will emotional intelligence help you understand the inspirational spirit? Well, herein, we'll focus on four elements culled from research. One major intelligent figure in this area of research is Daniel Goleman, who is probably most credited for popularizing the term *emotional intelligence*. With that said, and hopefully with respect paid, the four elements of emotional intelligence we'll focus on are self-awareness, self-management, social awareness, and relationship management.

First things first. **Self-awareness** is the most important concept of the four. Indeed, for me, this perspective comes from being a tireless follower, having a kaleidoscope of leadership responsibilities, and having trained more than 10,000 people in my Navy career. Self-awareness asks: Can you identify your feelings? What triggers you to have one of those four emotions I mentioned earlier? Use those answers to communicate and build relationships.

For example, I was placed in leadership positions almost immediately in my Navy career. I was probably 21 or 22 at the time. One of issues that troubled me most as a young leader was lying subordinates. When I knew my subordinates were lying, I would become incensed. They could have been lying to me about where they had been or about whether a task had been completed. I would immediately get blood-boiling angry if I knew they were lying. This was my trigger. Therefore, with a liar in my presence, I would make faces of disgust. My body language would be closed-off and tight. I might say something that was counterproductive to an already counterproductive situation. My initial response would almost certainly be to say something that wasn't conducive, given the conflict.

But, you see, that didn't help anyone. It didn't help the situation either. It didn't help my growth. However, once I recognized the error of my ways, my leadership transactions improved. The only source of knowledge is experience, according to Albert Einstein. Therefore, instead of making faces and engaging in poor non-verbal communication,

I would maintain a poker face, so to speak. I would hold eye contact. I would look at the liar in a comforting manner. I would listen intently. I would nod, illustrating understanding and comprehension of the– albeit creative–details of the lie. My physical reactions and non-verbal communication made for a far better interaction. My non-verbal behaviors acted as a disarmament condiment–peanut butter for the jelly to come. It makes sense now, considering what I learned in college. Our non-verbal communication is nearly 80% of what we communicate.

Do you remember the counterproductive language? The unconducive stuff? Instead of demeaning or devaluing the subordinate, from which nothing good ever came, I would calmly and matter-of-factly explain to the subordinate how his or her actions let down others. People tend to care more when they begin to understand (and appreciate) how their faults have multilateral implications, as opposed to unilateral consequences. For instance, I would tell him or her: "You know what? Because we couldn't find you, Johnny couldn't do his next task. He'll have to work later now. Oh yeah, Johnny had to wait for you to come back before he could go on lunch, too. Sorry, buddy, but none of us knew where you were. Maybe you want to go talk to Johnny and apologize." Do you see what I did here? Three things: I, one, explained physics, making the culprit understand his or her actions resulted in un-considered consequences; two, I removed myself from the power dynamic of our subordinate/peer relationship, switching the focus of the relationship to the by-products of the actions, the multiplier effect of it all, and the self-fulfilling need for redemption; and finally, (and here's the best part), I received a level of expected behavior from the subordinate without implicitly saying what I expected. Damn, I'm good! Your boy is nice! From my reaction, you've probably guessed that breakdown was the jelly. Okay, enough of the self-grandiosity. Sorry. But speaking of grade-A nutrition, here is some food for thought: Do you believe the word "why" played a part in any of my scenario? Email me your answer. I promise to respond.

Still, self-awareness is not exclusively tied to your own triggers. Self-awareness involves empathy and putting yourself in someone else's shoes. As a leader, you must allow yourself to see or experience things from someone else's perspective. You must ask yourself: How would I feel if that were me? In a nutshell, that's empathy. Yes, empathy. Empathy is a major component of leadership.

Another major component is the people we meet. Throughout your life and career, you'll have people who stand out to you as great leaders. Gene Peters, Boatswainmate Chief, U.S. Navy, was one of mine. Gene had remarkable empathy when it came to dealing with superiors, subordinates, and his peers. As a caveat, I should add that Gene falls into the category "people who are hurt the most are quite often most capable of healing." Nevertheless, Gene, my leadership G.O.A.T., modeled all the necessary empathetic behaviors, characteristics, and traits I would ever need. In case you don't know: G.O.A.T. = Greatest of All Time. Gene indoctrinated me with the concept of intrusive leadership. Instead, I'd like to think of it as involved leadership. Intrusive. Sounds bad, right? But it wasn't. Here's why: In my position, quite often I would have to counsel my subordinates on personal situations and family matters. It could be finance. It could be ramifications of divorce. It could be criminal matters. Yet, no matter what it was, Gene taught me to consider a "white glove" approach, which meant the matters took a certain level of discretion, delicacy, and diplomacy. For example, if it was a criminal matter, I would make sure the subordinate understood accountability for actions. I, however, managed subordinates as I wished to be managed. C'mon. You know when you've messed up. We all know when we've messed up. Yelling doesn't help. Scolding doesn't help. Ostracizing doesn't help. Many times, those actions feel like a "piling on" of an already difficult situation. I'm not saying you cannot be firm, but nuance has a place in these situations. Honestly, I feel like *nuance* is a dirty word these days. But I digress. What helps is empathy. Being honest helps. Keeping the lines of communication open helps. Following up on the needs and concerns of subordinates helps, as does being a good listener and allowing them to vent. Asking, "How can I help?" helps. Asking the question "What can you and I do to make sure this situation doesn't happen again?" helps. Many believe the opposite. Inevitably, though, what happens to us in our personal lives subconsciously affects our performance–whether we choose to believe it or not. Fact: You may never be in the position where you need to counsel individuals on this level, but this aptitude of self-awareness and empathy is vital nonetheless. It permeates other levels, like your ability to communicate and build relationships. Trust me. I know. Been there, done that sort of thing. Again, in the end, you're modeling good behavior for the next group of leaders, which is far more important than anything I'll discuss in this book.

Few things, however, are more important than **self-management**–managing yourself and controlling impulsive behavior. I remember the first time I saw self-management. Well, maybe not the first time. But it was MAJOR in terms of impact on my life. The imagery was as vivid as black and white.

Aw, yes, there I was in 2009. Slumdog Millionaire was hot, Rhianna disappeared from the Grammys for some reason, the Joker died, Tiger Woods kind of did too, Michael Phelps won another medal, Usain Bolt was fast, Parks and Recreation debuted, and Navy Seals made Captain Phillips a household name. Boring, boring year.

Early that year, President Obama gave his

nationally televised State of the Union Address. As you may know, during the State of the Union Address, presidents communicate their legislative agendas, the nation's economic outlook, and national priorities. That year, one of those priorities happened to be healthcare reform. During a section of the Address concerning Healthcare Reform, Joe Wilson, a Republican House member, shouted from his seat, "You lie," interrupting the president mid-speech. I was watching live, thinking, "Wow, this dude is gangster!" I mean, c'mon. The audacity. Did that just happen? Mind you this level of disrespect was–and still is–unheard of. In fact, if you Google this episode, you'll notice the *immediate* shock on the faces of those caught on camera, including those in the nearest vicinity of Obama. It was so bad it was all over the news the next day.

You're probably asking: What does this have to do with anything? I thought we were talking about self-management? Oh, but we are. We so are. Herein, the president could have reacted abruptly, with equal ignorance. He could have reacted in anger and with suggestive body language to match. He was just "called out" and "dissed" on live TV in front of millions of national and international viewers. Do you know what he did? He took a second, gathered himself, briefly closed his eyes and took a small breath simultaneously. Just like a singer–pick any singer–does right before he or she is about to hit that big note in a song.

In my anecdote, the proper self-managed response meant a more clearly communicated message, which meant a likelier rate of success in relationship-building with the receiver or receivers of the message, no matter how big the audience. This small anecdote is a big demonstration in self-management. The implications permeate. Perhaps it's why the protagonist in my anecdote won the Nobel Peace Prize the same year. The major lesson here: Don't be rash in your responses. Haste makes waste.

Speaking of waste, have I ever told you I'm not a big fan of meetings? Don't get me wrong. Meetings have a place. For most, however, that place is scheduled as a time-holder for "let me sound important" and unproductiveness. I guess I'm of the adage "don't use an axe when a scalpel will do." Don't schedule a meeting when an email or memo to one person will do. Make sure decision-makers are in the room. If they're not, then don't have the meeting. On a brighter note, and unthoughtful people aside, if you do find yourself in a meeting, you may find **social awareness** to be a desirable skill. Paying close attention to social habits is an investment with endless dividends. Done right, from a leadership standpoint, social awareness is one-part Art of War, one-part Confucianism, one-part mindfulness.

Here I go again…15 minutes early and waiting. Water bottle–got it. Pen and paper–full and free.

Talking points–rehearsed to memory. Seat raised to reasonable height to project confidence-- calibrated. Yet, seated in an area farthest from the head of the table. Nine o'clock in the morning comes. It's meeting time. Nobody here, of course. Late is the new black, apparently. Oops! Spoke too soon. One by one, attendees enter the room as if the recess bell just rang and everyone scatters into homeroom. Seated, I casually but astutely pay attention to meeting members as they enter the room. As each person walks-in, I'm clandestinely observe mannerisms and non-verbal language.

Kirk looks disheveled and down. Chrissy is jovial and is sharing micro-conversations with just about everyone in the room. Dan looks angry–better take note. Kim is quiet although appears well-prepared, looking copiously over her notes while writing in the margins. Oh, and then there's me. Did I mention I am the host of the meeting? "Hello, everyone!" As I say it, I scan the room, holding my eye contact for two to three seconds at Chrissy and Ted. Those two love sidebar conversations. My prolonged eye contact in their direction means: "Please stop talking and pay attention. We're beginning." After a brief introduction, agenda items and names of those responsible for each respective item are read. One task-orientated item is important, so I put it as the first item for discussion.

Several bodies are involved in this task, but Kim is one of the leads on this action item. Her primary partner, the other lead, is out sick. Nevertheless, Kim appears well-prepared. She begins and immediately does great. At the intersection of one of Kim's outlines, Dan says, "It won't work." He's not just disagreeing. He's disagreeable. Kim, to her credit, articulates a potential solution to his potential problem. Still in observation mode, by way of hyperawareness, I notice people appear galvanized around Kim as she covers this urgent matter. They lean forward in their chairs. Heads are nodding. Notes are being copiously written. Could Kim be a rising star? Is she earning their respect and admiration right before my eyes? Is Kim turning out to be more leader than manager? That last line is so important. I'm leveraging her for my next major project.

Not to be out-done, still, Dan finds comfort in contrarian tendencies. I notice others lean back. Faces become scourged. Attendees uncomfortably glance at each other with the, "is he serious?" face. Therefore, since I own the meeting: "Great, Dan. Let's parking lot some of those counterfactuals and/or speak offline." He replies, "Great idea!" Little does he know my aim is to keep the proper tone and comfort, inducing a productive environment going forward.

All settled, and discussion moved along, the group lands on the final agenda item. "Next item on the agenda–Chrissy, I believe this action item belongs to you?" Chrissy, quite loquacious at times, can go off on a tangent. In those instances, I find myself thinking, "I remember the first time I had a beer." Other members visibly tune out. Heads shift downward into phones. Side bars commence. Vital questions don't get asked, sacrificed for the sake of expediency. "Before you begin, Chrissy, I want to let you know you have 15 minutes. First, please let me hear from Kirk. Kirk, did you have any input?" Two things happened here: Chrissy is confined to being concise, and Kirk, who was disheveled and in la-la land, is now engaged. Why is that important? Because Kirk must be engaged and focused on this discussion due to the nature of his responsibilities with this assignment. If he is not paying attention, he may miss a crucial point.

The meeting ends. As meetings end, people shouldn't be consumed only with their own self-importance or how they came across in the meeting. If that had been me, I would have missed a valuable point. While exiting the space, I noticed an intern staring at me with withered hope in his eyes. I introduced myself. After small talk and demographical background exchanges, he says, "Sir, I have an idea." I reply, "Please don't call me Sir, I work for a living." It's an old Navy line. Anyway, I had noticed him listening attentively during the meeting, so I gave him my time. In his brief monologue, he provides a solution that was so good no one wanted to use it because no one could take credit for it, of course… duh. Months later, however, someone remembered the young man's suggestion and presented it as his or her own. The crowd cheered, applauded, and patted this individual on the back. Yes! I love when recognition is crushed. But that happens so seldom, I guess I shouldn't worry about it. Right? Lesson: It's a good thing I took a second to chat with him. Bridging that generational and power gap meant we were able to come up with a wider range of solutions to the business problem. Glad I too was paying attention.

Reading this book, raise your hand if you deal with difficult people. Okay, both hands raised– cool. If one of those difficult people is right next to you while you're reading this, you can put your hands down. I don't want to cause any trouble. I don't want the person next to you asking you why your hand is raised and you saying, "Uh…you!" Glad we understand cool is the rule. **Relationship management** involves managing conflicts, dealing with difficult people, and building rapport. That's not to say it's easy. With some people you just simply reach a saturation point. It's like, "Damn, I can't even deal." I'll be honest: I'm guilty. In those instances, I try to keep calm and carry on.

Still, people are investments; we have to curate relationships. Hopefully, that saturation point is never met. I remember being part of a workplace wellness program. During a session, a fellow member, a colleague, said: "It's important people ask themselves the question: Am I investing in people? Or in things?" I found his comment to be profound.

I thought back to my days in undergrad. I minored in communication, focusing on things like interpersonal skills.

Relationship-building is a big tent comprised of interpersonal skills, such as:

- Being a good listener
- Curating relationships
- Avoiding gossip (perhaps the hardest for some; I try hard not to, but others will pull you into their webs)
- Being positive
- Effective communication
- Appreciating others
- Asking often: "How can I help?" This question can be quite disarming
- Respect
- Trust

That last one, trust, is probably the most important to me. Please feel free to use your own accordingly. But I digress. While I was attending a seminar in Washington, D.C., a speaker who wrote a book on trust said, "Trust is fundamental to any good, productive working relationship." I agree 1000%.

The list above includes some of my personal favorites. But as my Spanish teacher would always say to me, "Renaldo, práctica, práctica, práctica."

Take time out of your day and every other day to speak with someone new. I truly do this even if I'm not necessarily fond of the individual. Herein, what you're doing is keeping an open line of communication. I especially made this my habit in the Navy. Why? Because terrible leaders often speak to subordinates only to reprimand. That's no way to lead. Therefore, if you keep the lines of communication somewhat open, you can more easily approach those disciplinary situations. It also helps the subordinates digest the conversation.

Relationship-building truly is about reaping what we sow, so to speak. I've seen the benefits of putting me in front of people I'd never thought I'd meet and going places I'd never thought I'd go. So, like the famous financial strategist Suze Orman always says, "People first, then things."

Enough. Enough. Why should you care? Why should you be an emotionally intelligent leader? Here's why. There's *why* again. Where was I? Yes, advantages. The Carnie Institute of Technology studied financial success and human engineering and found that 85% of financial success is related to emotional intelligence and only 15% to technical knowledge.

I'm not done yet. Let's say your boss doesn't appreciate emotional intelligence. He or she looks at EQ as a buzzword or fluff. If that's true, he or she doesn't understand business, time, money, and resources. Question: How much do you think workplace issues, productivity and conflict among them, cost businesses every year? You're not even close. Guess higher. Per Entrprenuer.com, when CPP Inc.–publishers of the Myers-Briggs Assessment and the Thomas-Kilmann Conflict Mode Instrument–commissioned a study on workplace conflict, they found that, in 2008, US employees spent 2.8 hours per week dealing with conflict. This amounts to approximately $359 billion in paid hours (based on average hourly earnings of $17.95), or the equivalent of 385 million working days.

Study after study shows factors of EQ increase productivity and decrease workplace conflicts and complaints in business. Looks like it'll save you a few pennies too.

I'll end the advantages with this: It's important to understand your strengths and weaknesses. One of my favorite quotes comes from Shakespeare, who famously said, "A fool believes himself to be wise, but a wise man knows himself to be a fool." Being mindful and present equals a high mental capacity, which helps formulate perspective, which helps formulate decision-making.

Are you ready for the bad news?

No one ever wants the bad news. C'mon, am I right?

You never hear people say: "We want more bad news. We want more!" For instance, you go to the car dealer and see all the nice options. The dealer is constantly harping on all of the good features, good feature after good feature. You're smiling, listening, and loving it. Then, the dealer starts talking price, payment, maintenance cost, and costs for "extra features." You're thinking: "Stop. Let me stop you right there, buddy. On second thought, do I *really* need this car?" You don't want to hear what he is saying. It's bad news.

Being emotionally unintelligent is bad news, or disadvantageous. One disadvantage is that your job may be in danger. We live so close to our own lives that we don't see the ways in which our behavior and character can, and does, kill the morale of those around us. With that said, in your case, if subordinates, colleagues, or teammates cannot work well with you, they will leave, mentally or physically. Similarly, management will make an effort, clandestine or publicly, to see you removed.

One thing that always moves me is how many people are extremely book smart yet not people smart. Do you know anyone who fits this profile? I'm guessing you do. These folks are extremely book smart but lack people skills (or maybe commons sense too). Focusing on and leveraging EQ is the antidote. In its absence, you could very well be hurting relationship-building, communication, leadership, problem-solving, and your career trajectory.

Actionable steps you can take:

- Be self-aware
- Know your emotions and what triggers (HUGE)
- Keep an open sense of perspective
- Be aware of what Aristotle said: "We are what we repeatedly do"
- Grab hands with someone and dance

Looking up as if to the sky for advice, he climbs a dozen-plus steps until he reaches the top of the platform. Minor hypertension overcomes him. While taking deep breaths, he closes his eyes to control any inertia of chest palpitations. Eyes still closed, he flashes back to childhood memories. It was the time he climbed the roof of "Hot Spot," the local candy store. The building was easily the tallest building in the world, from his young perspective. The fear and wave of emotions felt the same now as it did then. His eyes open. "Next, you're up," a voice yells. He walks step-by-step to the edge of platform, as if he's counting off the square feet in a room. Now to the edge, he walks back a step, takes a deep breath. Now a step forward, back to the edge. He wiggles his toes along the edge for grip to the beat of his heart as it drops to his stomach. "It's just water kid," the instructor says. "You ready?"

Not so fast, my friend

"Motivation is more than the carrot or the stick"

R. Edward Freeman of the Darden School of Business at the University of Virginia

I'm listening to a YouTube video featuring the professor during the final semesters of my MBA program. The professor is rehashing a story set at Harvard University. Mr. Freeman tells the tale of Harry Levinson, who, from Levinson's bio, was an American psychologist and consultant in work and organizational issues. He was a pioneer in the application of psychoanalytic theory to management and leadership. Mr. Freeman tells the tale of how Mr. Levinson would hang out at the Harvard Business School, mingling, sharing dialogue, and generally fraternizing with business types. Mr. Freeman describes to the audience an image Mr. Levinson drew. The illustration includes a half-oval linear shape with a carrot on one side and a stick on the other. In the middle of this image is a question mark. Mr. Levinson asks those in attendance at Harvard, "So, what animal do you assume to be in the middle between the carrot and stick?" These individuals, whom I assume are the best and brightest, say, "A jackass!" However, prior to the drawing and before he asks the previous question, he asks those same individuals this question first: "What motivates employees?" To this, they answer: "rewards and punishment." Or, to put it differently, a carrot or a stick. Perhaps lost in Mr. Freeman's corky and witty veneer is an invaluable lesson. To no fault of his own, he attempts to drive home his point in a video relegated to two minutes; that's like explaining America's race problems in 140 characters.

Where was I? The morale of his story is this: The factors that motivate and engage humans are more complicated than rewards and punishment.

In my personal and professional experience, more often than not, poor leaders have a binary motivational framework. Poor leaders leverage this theoretical underpinning; however, they fail to grasp one of my favorite words absent in society today: *nuance*. Pretty sure it's a dirty word, that old nuance. Pretty sure it's almost as dirty of a word as *critical-thinking*.

Not to worry, my friend. In the next chapter, Engaging the Disengaged, the dirty words and residual residue are cast aside. You will have a better conceptualization of how nuance and motivational factors are tangential. You will see that people are more than jackasses. You will see, to Mr. Freeman's point, that people are complex.

ENGAGING THE DISENGAGED

Let's start from the beginning. Once considered a buzz word, *fluff*, or "touchy-feely management," *engagement* is one of the most critical challenges leaders face. Leaders have more recently come to the realization that engagement matters. And winter is coming. That's a quick Game of Thrones reference. Dragons are real. Now that we got "I'm a bit of a nerd" out the way, let's proceed.

Ask yourself the question: Does my business, organization, or team believe I'm engaged? I bet you probably answered with a "yes." You totally may be engaged. I'm not arguing that fact. In fact, on this topic I conduct live seminars to fairly large audiences. Every time, I ask the audience, "Who in here feels like your organization looks at you as engaged? Please raise your hand." No lie. Ninety percent of the hands raise. Yet, what we think and what polls show prove both are not remotely aligned. According to reports, 70% of US workers are not reaching their full potential, by being either "not engaged" or "actively disengaged."

So, what does that mean? What are the implications?

It means employee engagement is the most important challenge for leaders, dwarfing many other concerns. Present reader excluded (cough) of course, now that we know most people are not as engaged as once thought, we can dive into some of the **problems**, **causes**, and **solutions**.

Indeed, disengagement corresponds to a lack of performance and productivity. That's a problem. Big problem. We know a connection between engagement and performance exists; a more engaged employee means a more productive employee. Consequently, research represents what many already know: Organizations, teams, and business are losing substantial productivity and/or profit.

As a leader, you must be mindful. Engagement affects the figurative health of your organization. You're not getting your best output. Engagement is "out of shape"; the organizational cardio is no good. Employee engagement impacts what *you* or *they* do and how *you* or *they* do it.

Taking a different approach, one question I find people have with engagement is: What does *it* look like? People essentially ask, "Ron, where is the picture I can trace?" Some questioners probably couldn't trace their own hands, which brings back memories. I remember being a kid at Thanksgiving. Teachers would have all the students trace their hands. Courtesy of some paste and colored markers, our traced hands miraculously turned into images of turkeys. I'd get excited, take mine home to mom, and five minutes later it's in the trash (single tear, right eye). Terrible lady.

I joke. I kid. She'd at least hold it for 48 hours. Sure mom. You're taking it to work to show your friends.

All this talk of tracing and hands got me to thinking. Speaking of hands, have you ever heard of the "invisible hand" in economics? This is a concept birthed by Adam Smith, author of *The Wealth of Nations*, which many consider the bible of capitalism. The "invisible hand" is described by Smith as an unseen force or mechanism that guides individuals to unwittingly benefit society through pursuit of their private interests. Irrespective of how you feel about economic philosophy, could *he* very easily be describing engagement? Think about that for a second. Maybe the answer will become clearer at the end of the chapter. Guess you have to wait and see. I know. I know. The suspense is killing me too.

Try another concept on for size. You know what an obscenity is, right? Go ahead. Please describe it for me. Better yet, since I'm not there, please describe it to yourself aloud, preferably in a public place. Public places get my creative juices flowing. You always hear and see the most interesting things. No, not a good idea, you say. Okay. No worries. Hall passes accepted. Obscenity. Yes.

The Supreme Court–perhaps you've heard of it–was asked in 1964 to define and explain an obscenity, in the landmark case *Jacobellis v. Ohio*. During the review, Justice Potter Stewart describe an obscenity by saying, "You know it when you see it," coining the now famous phrase. Could *he* very easily be describing engagement?

Academia will tell you, "Only through surveys can only truly tell if you or your employees are engaged." That's nice. I disagree a bit. There is an eyeball test. There are mitigating factors. There is nuance. Indeed, for that matter, whether it's the invisible hand or knowing it when you see it, the problem with engagement is that, if we can't identify it, it is harder to model and judge on a Likert Scale.

From a leadership perspective, let's discuss some causes related to poor employee engagement and see why 70% of US workers may not be working at or near optimal performance levels.

1) Issues with Management

Herein, we need to consider a couple of things. First, an old cliché. You may have heard people say, "People quit bosses, not jobs." I remember one of my professors commenting on this very premise in an economic course. But if you don't believe me, you can read a ton of articles embracing the said notion. For example, I remember reading a Forbes article; it was something about "Employees

Versus Management" and the real reasons employees leave. The study usually works like this: Researchers poll mangers and subordinates of companies, asking managers why they believe employees leave. Researchers then ask employees the real reason why they quit their jobs. In most cases, what they find, research shows, is that managers believe employees leave for things like better pay, advancement, bonuses, and ambition. What the research shows is employees really jump ship because of lousy bosses–negativity, lack of recognition, uncomfortable feelings, and a lack of inspiration. Interesting enough, it usually doesn't matter whether it's Fortune 500 company or "mom & pop" shop. The results tend to be reliable. The important point to remember: Please don't allow naiveté to blur your vision.

Bullying is another issue affecting the relationship with management. Research shows bullying affects employees' health and ability to concentrate. Bullying can also make the environment one of fear and disrespect. As you may know, bullying comes in all shapes and sizes. Pay close attention to bullying in the forms of sexually harassment, workplace clicks, and underrepresented groups.

My personal favorite is the abominable "no man." Not sure what the abominable "no-man" is? "Hi, boss, I have a great idea and here's a specific, actionable, and measurable way we can do it. Are you interested?" The "no man" says, "No." "Here's a way we can increase engagement and employee recognition. Are you interested boss?" The "no man" says, "No." "Boss, do humans need water to survive? The "no man" says, "No, that won't work." As you may have noticed, the abominable "no man" leader is fixated on the word "no." His or her actions and responses are either the result of fear-based, risk-adverse workplace tendencies, or simply arrogance. Either way, as a result, the leader this describes will divest champions of innovation. Staff, teammates, and subordinates will be uninspired and unengaged, all because they don't feel vested in their organizations.

Finally, we come to the Big Five Factor Model of personality types, which is often described using the acronym O.C.E.A.N.–*openness, conscientiousness, extraversion, agreeable, neuroticism*. A core section of one of my MBA classes was entirely devoted to the Big Five Factor Model. I'm being facetious somewhat; however, we did have great discussions and papers requiring critical thought concerning its relevance. More importantly, first, I must give respect to the founders and forebears whom we can thank for understanding said personality traits. Names includes Paul Costa, Robert R. McCrae, Warren Norman, Ernest Tupes, Raymond Cattell, J.M. Digman, and Lewis Goldberg.

So, what's the so what, as they say? …

Well, if you have a leader who is an abominable "no man," someone who is closed off to try new activities and/or is less amenable to change, then an employee or athlete prone to openness and innovation may find conflict in this relationship. Both parties are remarkably polar opposites. Therefore, some give-and-take is required, or the relationship will end at a saturation point.

In the case of the conscientiousness type, the leader may be thorough, time-orientated, and goal- driven. What if a subordinate has a *laissez-faire* mentality? While discussing outcomes and deliverables, she says, "Hey, chill-lax we'll get to it when we get to it." What if she's habitually late meeting appointments and deadlines? In this example, a conflict will most certainly occur due to variance and levels of expected behaviors. Perhaps you'll even call her a *millennial*. Oh my!

Not enough excitement? I'll raise you an extrovert. This example is easy: "My name is Ron. I'm a leader. I'm a curmudgeon. I'm a leader. I'm introverted. Most of my staff, nevertheless, are extroverts. I got this job only because my skill set is technically sound, and I've been here longer than my colleagues. Did I mention I hate Mondays? Monday morning. First thing. Employees line up outside my office just to tell me about their *entire* weekend. Did I mention they're really outgoing, always developing social activities inside and outside of work? Great. Nothing could go wrong within the confines of my interactions, right?" Wrong. One more thing: If this is you, there's a solid chance staff are calling you a pill behind your back. But then again, you're an introvert, so nobody cares. Now, please go away. Go on. Go on.

Depending on the situation, an agreeable personality type might succumb to my humble request in the previous sentence. I'm always managing expectations. Ah, yes, the agreeable personality type. The agreeable types are great people. Leaders love agreeable personality types. Leaders love "yes men." Leaders love feeling like they're always right. Leaders love being adorned. We all know these types of leaders; they remind me of Ralphie in the classic American movie *A Christmas Story*. It's the scene where Ralphie daydreams of an A+ on his homework assignment. Ralphie's teacher and fellow classmates shower him with amazement and adulations. The applause echoes like the Roman Coliseum in the days of the gladiator. Ralphie basks in the glow, representative of the leaders we know.

Wait a second.

What if you're not like Ralphie? What if you don't like "yes men"? What if you believe the best solutions are derived from a healthy amount of conflict? What if you want people who will challenge you to think outside your box or myopathy? Sorry to tell you, agreeable personality types are probably not the ones you want around come decision-making time. I'm just saying. In fact, you hear this with athletes a lot. Sports journalist and talking heads will say, "She got into trouble because everyone around her was afraid to tell her 'no,' so she kept going down the wrong path." Newsflash: It happens in business too. Something to consider, perhaps?

I've managed literally thousands of people across the human spectrum. Some good. Some bad. Some ugly. Perhaps managing neuroticism is as close to kryptonite as I've come, not to say I'm Superman or anything. What did you say? I am your Superman? Thank you. Are you trying to Ralphie me? If so, I accept. You're far too kind. Since you've been innocently introduced to Ralphie, if you've seen A Christmas Story, you'll know Ralphie's character is profiled as neurotic. From my experience, backed by research, neurotic personality types exhibit episodes of "paralysis by analysis," emotionally insular or erratic behavior, and idiosyncrasies. What happens when you're the neurotic leader? Uh huh…yes, me. You may be the neurotic leader. You may be the neurotic subordinate or athlete. Your mind may be a raging fire. So, on the other side of that, you must focus on the revolution in training and processes of emotional intelligence. Indeed, it is the reason the chapter on emotional intelligence foreshadows this one. Yes, Sir, that's how I survive as a neurotic: reminding myself to not allow the process to become the punishment.

2) Trust & Faith in Organizational Leadership

According to a report from ToleroSolutions, 45% of employees say lack of trust in leadership is the biggest issue impacting work performance. Employees want to trust, believe, and feel leaders care about them, personally and professionally. For me, trust is, unquestionably, a must. My trust issues with managers have always stemmed from recognizing their ulterior motives–to gossip, to seeing me as a threat as opposed to an ally, among other things.

On a macro level, distrust within an organization can have a devastating multiplier effect. For instance, a lack of trust and faith can quickly become contagious. It's mutually assured destruction. It starts with four words and a four-letter acronym: cover your own a$$ (CYOA). Imagine if everyone in your organization felt this way. Imagine if Michael Jordan could not trust his teammates to help on defense. Imagine if Serena Williams didn't trust her father to have the best intentions in mind. Imagine if Warren Buffet didn't have his trusted partner, Charlie Munger, for advice and reconciliation.

Sadly, I've been in environments supremely inadequate with trust, where nothing gets done. I have watched the stagflation in the form of an uncanny delicate dance. Imagine you have the world's most advanced train with no tracks to reach its intended destinations.

3) Feeling Personal Accomplishment

Simply put, if there's no thanking, appreciation, or habits of amplifying accomplishments, then there's "no there there." Not enough there. Storied research backs this claim. Perhaps you've heard of Maslow's Hierarchy of Needs. Maslow, a pioneer in psychology, theorized that humans carry a set of innate needs. Most illustrations depict his hierarchy of human needs in the form of a pyramid. At the pyramid's apex, which indicates the most important need for humans, is self-esteem, with which I'm sure you are familiar, and self-actualization. Merriam-Webster defines *self-actualization* as fully realizing one's potential. Therefore, if a leader's environment doesn't consist of recurring feedback, intrinsic and/or extrinsic reward, and the recognition of good behaviors, that leader is failing not only organizational performance and productivity but also the human experience concurrently. Is that deep enough there?

One one thousand, two one thousand, three one thousand, and four. Stretching: The most boring but necessary act in the pre-game. Considering his present circumstances, he knew he had to stretch well. The team he was getting ready to face was a regional powerhouse, and he would be matching up with one of the top-ranked guards in the nation. The stands were full. Patrons were anxiously stuffing their faces with soda, popcorn, and candy, anticipating a prized fight. Whistles went off all around the surrounding dome, albeit seemingly unnoticed. You could call it white noise.

His subconscious thoughts circulate.

Are his shoes new enough? He'll need excellent grip. Is he strong enough? Anatomically, this team is more NFL than NBA. Will his coaches and teammates believe in him? Will his coaches and teammates trust his decisions? Will his basketball I.Q. help him pass one of many final exams on the court? College coaches, scouts, and recruiters will be grading the aesthetics of each exam.

He goes into the bathroom and paces back and forth like a lion in a cage. Out of the bathroom, the game is a quick drink of Gatorade from the beginning. His starting five hits the court and daps up the competition. He takes his place, pre-tip off. His entire body feels like a finger nail bent back too far. He holds his knees, bent over, looking up and forward at the star guard across from him. Just then, a mirage of realism happens; the lights dim, walls enclose, and the ceiling freefalls.

When I am lecturing on engagement, somewhere around this point, I would orchestrate an activity. In the immortal words of Will Ferrell: "It's provocative. It gets the people going." I do that because I'm transitioning to the solutions. After a smooth transition sentence, I'll ask people to think of some tasks, behaviors, or responsibilities that energize them. What I'm doing in this exercise is manipulating them into being mindful. You can find many definitions and examples of mindfulness on the internet; however, the goal of my manipulation is to get participants to use their brains in the quality or state of being conscious or aware of something.

I do this because…surprise, the brain is amazing!

Subsequently, I point out to the participants the importance of the activity. But first, I explain the frontal lobe, which consists of emotions and behavioral control; and the sensory cortex, which manages sensation and brain arousal. I tell them, "As a matter of fact, when you engage in the activities you thought of, within the pleasure center of your brain, the pituitary gland releases beta-endorphins that can increase feelings of trust and bonding."

For you as the leader, and you as the individual, my activity has a reciprocal and mutually beneficial aim. Yes, I'm asking you to be mindful personally. I'm asking you also to be mindful of others. More to come in the next paragraphs concerning the importance of being mindful of others. Back to my point. Right now, I'm speaking directly to you. If you're not engaged, I'll bet a nice wager that your people, teammates, or contemporaries won't be either.

So, as a result, be mindful. Turn those energizers into

action items. What activities get you excited? How can you infuse these activities into items for your job? Maybe it's baking. Maybe it's event-planning. For example, I had a boss who loved organizing events and planning activities; she loved everything from doing events for holidays to organizing fun and games at corporate retreats. The people-watcher I am, I noticed that she glowed and radiated while organizing and during the activities. If you looked close enough, you could see endorphins oozing from her like penumbras–all because that's what she loves to do. Event-planning and coordinating are her energizers; she's drawing from a deep well. In her case, in terms of engagement (happiness too), it's important at work and in life to look for areas to leverage said activities. Sure, you're not her. Maybe for you it's brainstorming. Maybe it's simply being nice. I like being nice; I even like killing mean people with kindness. Circling back a bit. In the end, like my story on Adam Smith's economic invisible hand theory, your energized, engaged part is affecting the whole. Positively. Or negatively. Does that make sense?

Photosynthesis CO_2+ $2H_2O$ + Light = CH_2+O_2+H_2O

Probably before you even knew what science was, you were taught photosynthesis. Perhaps your teacher or parent explained photosynthesis to you in an elementary, nursery-rhyme style fashion. In a nutshell, photosynthesis is the process by which plants make energy. In a supply chain manner, the plant leverages the sun, water it receives, and carbon dioxide in the atmospheres to produce sugar, which in essence is energy and/or food for the plant life. What's even cooler is that, if you can read this book and are learning about photosynthesis for the first time now, I have a really great bridge with scenic views I can sell you for a steal of a price. Really. Please inquire within.

Now that you have taken my pants and shirt, please allow me to explain, through the process of photosynthesis, how being mindful as a leader will improve engagement and talent-development.

Ladies and gentlemen, the story you are about to read is true. However, the names have been changed to protect the innocent. Meet Seamen Jones and Smith. These two were Dennis the Menace squared. Both would go absent at times. Their work assignments would go uncompleted or completed with substandard care. Although they were trustworthy; you could always count on speaking to them concerning respect, military-bearing, and appearance issues. Others in leadership and I had initially projected their trajectory as a troubled arc. In this story, however, the fate of power means accepting things you normally wouldn't consider. To that end, I began to water the seeds. First, I knew both had the capacity for intelligence, so I let the sun in, letting them put that untapped energy to work. I put my pride aside. I invited their innovation and thoughts, whereas before they wanted to do side projects–or CO_2– germane to our work. I was an abominable "no man." This time, considering time, money and resources, I tapped their creativity on projects, to gauge how they could contribute to a better result. In fact, I began to see them form into flowers, so to speak, as I let them take charge in the areas of search-and-rescue setup, amphibious operations, and replenishment at sea. Frequent and consistent communication of the vision was a key strategy, of course. As both grew, I facilitated their full development by defining realistic and achievable goals. The new autonomy had more desirable results than we could have ever imagined. Both blossomed. Both were more motivated to learn. Both turned out exceptionally well. Both ended up turning into "star players" within our unit.

Yoda might say, "Inclusive leadership, that is."

Aww…but the confections we see…

The talent development and maturation that came to fruition was sweet. In the midst of everything, I mathematically incubated that "whole trust and relationship with manager" thing I mentioned earlier. Do you remember my problem of what engagement looks like? We saw it with Seamen Jones and Smith. To a larger extent, there was an eyeball test. We could recognize engagement. Both Smith and Jones became energetic and prideful problem-solvers and team players. A big change occurred before my eyes. They seemed to be more flexible and trusting.

Here's a recap: I want to make sure the lessons learned are clear. Trust me. I didn't forget; you're grasping photosynthesis for the first time today. In the anecdote, I used my vision and power for empowerment, enabling my subordinates to make decisions, solve problems, and set goals. Herein, leadership must have a conceptual understanding of addition by subtraction. The political will to hold onto unnecessary power and may inasmuch affect the growth of the whole. Or, as Linda Hill, a Harvard Business faculty member, so eloquently stated, "Those with position power are responsible for creating contexts in which others can lead and flourish."

Recognition! Recognition! Read all about it!

According to experts and researchers, recognition is the Number 1 force behind employee engagement. Recognition is paramount to motivating and retaining employees.

I learned some great lessons concerning acknowledgment from Dr. Kevin "Doc" Marbury. When I meet Doc, he was at Old Dominion University and president of the National Intramural-Recreation Sports Association (NIRSA). Doc started as my mentor in NASPA, a national fellowship program aimed at getting disenfranchised groups into the many fields of higher education. He's been a father figure ever since. Currently, Doc is the Vice-President for Student Life at the University of Oregon. Without ever opening his, or anyone else's wallet, Doc was absolutely amazing at recognition, acknowledging my worth, and building my self-confidence. Doc is definitely one of the faces on my Mount Rushmore of leadership.

Therefore, if you're a leader, don't fool or lull yourself into believing the only recognition employees appreciate has tax implications. Leaders must find those transactions where they can inject and meet the intrinsic needs of others. For instance, in the case of athletes, much of your recognition comes in the form of intrinsic reward unless, and or until, you are competing professionally.

I love giving acknowledgment for a task completed. I try to be a serial acknowledger. One thing being a serial acknowledger does is it make critiques and criticism easier. The more I interact and communicate, the more fluid relationships feel. The more fluid relationships feel, the easier it is to have those tough conversations. It's like this: Have you ever had a boss or coach who gives feedback only when a he or she has something negative to say? I know. This never happens, right? But just in case it does someday, please keep reading. Also, don't be the leader who does not give positive feedback for a fallacy-filled fear that it will come back to haunt you at rating time or during performance review. C'mon. If this is you, you're being a poor leader. Don't hurt the 80% for the 10% or 20%. In all my work and athletic experience, I have never had acknowledgement detrimentally hurt me or the mission. Here, your ambition to create a culture of engagement must outweigh your fear.

Part of building a culture ripe with engagement means leaders face silos of relationships, networks, and interdependencies. Inspiration, optimism, and positivity are great characteristics toward that end. I hate to gloat, but I was a pretty decent basketball player. My position was point guard, the player on the floor who does most of the ball-handling. Over the years, I've played with and against some amazing talent. Some of my teammates and opponents went to the NBA, and others played in professional leagues all over the world. One thing I learned early as a point guard, the position that many perceive as the coach on the floor, was the application of encouragement. For example, sometimes during a game, I would notice a teammate lacked focus or wasn't as engaged as usual; he might appear lost or awry. So, as a result, since I handled the ball regularly, I would make sure he touched the ball next time down court. I might call a specific play for him. I wanted to get my disengaged teammate involved in the action. I might high-five him or slap him on the rear, which in sports is recognition for something well-done. During a break in the game, I'd tell him a joke that I knew would make him laugh. My goal was to reignite his focus. My goal was to get him to pass my eyeball test. Ninety percent of the time, my actions worked. The player would go from lamb to lion. Here's the best part: It's systems-thinking once again, because you're only as strong as your weakest link. I told you I was good.

What I did was nothing new. In fact, John Quincy Adams, the sixth president of the United States, once said: "If your actions inspire others to dream more, do more and become more. You are a leader." Positive leaders arrange a high bar for followers, providing motivation and inspiration concurrently. Not surprisingly, a Robbins & Judge survey in 2016 found that 66% of US employees mentioned positive appreciation as a prime motivator. Conversely, a professor taught me that one negative comment equates to five positive comments. It's not exactly empirical evidence, but it makes sense. I still remember the terrible things you said about me in the third grade, Carl. If I see you, Carl, it's on!

Carl didn't value me, but you definitely want to recognize those who embody the values to which you or your mission aspire. For example, the Navy's core values are honor, courage, and commitment. Here's an example of pinpointing those who demonstrate those values: If Seaman Jones and Seaman Smith demonstrated a staunch commitment to an operation, I made sure to recognize their efforts publicly. In fact, when I received awards, like time-off awards or something similar, for Jones' and/or Smith's work, I often would deflect and recognize them, or entirely give the award to them. Now, not only am I doing a selfless thing, I'm *also* demonstrating a continuation of two values, honor and courage.

Also, don't forget. Remember that leadership–it's about your people, not you. Fight for your people. When it's time for awards, fight for the highest level of awards possible. Put the pressure on management to talk you down or decrease the levels of the awards. What poor leaders don't get is this: You can't expect your people to fight for you when you never fight for them. Trust me, your employees (or players) know whether you really care about them.

That message is a jewel, by-the-way.

Need more evidence?

My corporation's values are teamwork, effectiveness, and accountability. With that said, one time I worked on maybe the most boring and laborious project ever. I worked with a small group of colleagues; I ran the point. I should add that, at the time, all my colleagues assigned to the project out-ranked me. Long story short, the project was a success. After the completion of the project, I wrote awards for the group, sent them up the chain, and the awards were subsequently approved. I have to be honest, the project was hardly recognized as front-page material, but it aligned with our company's values: teamwork, effectiveness, and accountability. In both examples, those of the Navy and corporate America, I reinforced core values. In both cases, after my colleagues received their formal recognition, I couldn't stop those colleagues from asking me whether I needed additional help elsewhere, even if I tried; they became over-accommodating, which was really cool. I guess it's like they say, "Never feed a stray cat, because if you do, they'll keep coming back." All joking and analogies aside (cough), one could argue these individuals were starving for recognition. And we all have to eat to live.

Alright. You have everything you need. The rest is easy; you'll be turning water into wine in no time. Now get out there and make magic. What should you remember?

Okay. Okay. I will end this chapter with some action items. On an individual level, remember to be mindful, not just as an individual but as a manger and an organization. The tree limbs and by-products extend wide.

Focus on what energizes you. In which areas can you allow others to be energized? Am I, or are we, investing in "idea fusion"?

Also, curate relationships. "You don't have to get in shape if you stay in shape!" I told you I was coming back to that analogy. Remember, relationships are dynamic. Work at them. They traject teambuilding, a culture of trust, and workplace excellence.

On an organizational level, build a culture and atmosphere conducive and ripe for spreading the pathogens of engagement. We totally want to see an epidemic. Ground zero might look like a rewards-and-recognition program that has a pulse. You may unconsciously create an environment in which people start helping one another, fixing problems sooner with more coordination. People will believe more in problem-solving than blame, which, if you didn't know, is considered Eastern business philosophy leverage by companies like Toyota.

Remember to encourage recurring feedback. General Electric, by way of Jack Welch, whom many consider the architect of the industrial performance system, practices the annual review as religion. Now leaders at General Electric—arguably blasphemy—are considering changing to a model of recurring feedback, believing it incubates a culture that emphasizes constant improvement and individual success.

Hopefully you were able learn something from this chapter. In this chapter, I tried to give you some anatomy, economic theory, law, workout advice, and sci-fi. I was on a roll. No whammies! I'm super dating myself with the whammy reference, too.

Anyway, finally, I want to leave you with this: The emphasis should not be about satisfaction but improvement.

The scurried shuffle of shoes stops as pair after pair meets its intended destination. What sounds like random thumps from fists hitting a punching bag come from the desk; the rest of the backpacks fall to the floor. Facing forward in military fashion at attention, the once-animated and boisterous bodies grow silent. The silence was predicated from what was to come.

The one in charge, otherwise known as the professor, walked in curmudgeonly. Heads look around trying to make sense, looking for validation for something no one knew. Mixed facial expressions and big eyes have taken hostage of the room. As the professor walks to each pair of shoe-occupied desks, he places an item in hand. Deflation, lip smacks, and uncomfortable giggles occur randomly, destination after destination.

The leader stops at a corner destination secured firmly in the back, avoids eye contact, and places down an item. D+ circled in bright Corvette red. Deflation. Anger. Hopelessness lay stagnant at this target. Next, the feet in those shoes "went to sleep." The tingle in the hands followed. This target blacked out. But not until after the ringing in both ears.

YOU GOT SKILLS

You are afraid. I too was afraid. Only *I* offer a promise. What you are reading is a promise. It is a promise to help you tap your untapped potential, because your potential is unlimited. My goal is for all fancy words and witty commentary to act as your standard operating procedure, battle plan, game plan, or ship's course. But in the end, "The power is yours!" That's a quick Captain Planet reference. Great cartoon. Seriously. Solid plots. Well-written scripts. Diverse and inclusive casting. Anyway, speaking of the winds of change, in this chapter I'll explain obstacles preventing you from being the best leader you can possibly be and how you can overcome them.

Before we start, I need a promise from you: 100% honesty as you read along and lead into the future.

Ok?

Good.

Let me tell you a story about my first year of undergrad as a veteran. When school started, the first time I walked on campus, I was nervous as hell. Big buildings in every direction. Maps pointed me in the wrong way. I didn't know anyone. All these students scurrying about. People talking on their phones, not paying attention. Clothes were obnoxiously bright. And everyone was wearing skinny jeans.

During that first semester, I had a statistics class. Math is something I will not say I miss. I was never like: "Oh, you love math. Great. Me too!" Back to my story. Here I am in stats class, head down, sad and depressed as the professor gives us a run-down of the syllabus. All I heard was Charlie Brown's teacher, "WAH WAH WAHHH." Just listening to him speak, I may have snapped a pencil in half between my fingers from the anxiety. It gets better. As the professor details all the *fun* we will have with numbers this semester, nerds were all around me saying, "This class is going to be *so* easy." Maybe a surprise to no one reading now, but nerds had merged their way into the cool lane, which was absolutely another shock to my system. So, yea, when did nerds become part of the cool crowd? Missed that. I found the nerds in class more embodied, opinionated, and confident than I last remembered. I'm telling you, it was too much. Too much.

Days turned into weeks. Weeks turned into the first exam. Indeed, minus my self-limiting beliefs, I had been coasting. I did fairly well on the homework assignments. The professor, to his credit, had a small exam review session in class prior to the test. I grasped the material once and was over and done with it. Your brain learns to remove unnecessary information from the mind, kind of thing. My actions and concerns for the test continued haphazardly until the day of the test.

A week or more had passed. I'm was on pins and needles waiting for the results. "Boy, this professor must be really lazy if he takes this long to grade 20 or so exams." Being as ignorant as one could be. Next class, the professor walked in and said, "Here are your graded exams." He held them outstretch in the air like Simba, the Lion King, at birth. Professor walked the aisles, putting them down with robotic speed and precision. Once I got mine, I figured the grade was bad as soon as he handed it to me face-down. I flipped over the paper. Damn. The grade was terrible. I was sick. He left the homie on stuck.

The next day, I picked up my face and the rest of myself from the floor. The day before, I was too upset to enjoy anything. The red score on my paper crowded my thoughts. I remember thinking, "Damn. I'm going to fail this class." The stages of grief had me asking: "Who does this guy think he is? How could he have done this to me? Didn't he see how hard I was trying?"

I went to his office during the office hours prescribed in the syllabus, but I had emailed him to make an appointment, to let him know I would be coming. I knocked on the door. He answered: "Come in and take a seat. What can I do for you?"

I said: "Thanks for seeing me, Sir. But I'm confused with this score. I'm not sure how I did so bad."

Turning and straightening up in his chair, he says, "Let me see that." I had the paper, covered in red ink, in hand. I should have taken the test in red ink instead of pencil. It definitely would have matched his décor and gave my test a more monochromatic feel. He took the paper from me.

I watched him feel his way through my exam. I watched him make non-verbal confirmation or confused gestures, as if he gave a damn. "Well, it seems pretty clear to me," he said. I took back my paper. Mute. Unsure of mental and physical time.

I guess I was hoping for: "Aw, Ron. Yes, I made several mistakes in grading your paper. Let's make this right. Here's an A."

To make things worse, he said, "You'll probably end up with a D+ or C – in my course. But you got the score you got." I won't say how I was really feeling and what I was really thinking, because I'm classy. However, imagine how you might feel in a similar circumstance, but add a reasonable 10,000 on the anger meter.

Come here. Closer. Sshhh. Here's a secret most leaders don't know: Good leaders understand a time to follow. The great ones understand when and how.

Rage and hurt aside, I was knocked down, but as the late, great Green Bay Packers Coach Vince Lombardi once said, "It's not whether you get knocked down, it's whether you get up." Something inside me sparked a chain of events. Immediately after my conversation with the professor, I contacted the tutor assigned to our class. I worked with her religiously in-person or via email. I teamed with one of my great friends, Eric. We studied together. I made him test my comprehension. We ate a lot of wings and drank a lot of refreshments, too. I was tenacious. With each new lesson, I would practice the homework, formulas, and equations over and over and over. They say repetition is the key to success. I'd go out on a date with my wife, and as soon as we got home, I might test myself on the correlation coefficient.

Guess what happened.

I aced my way through the professor's comments and his class. I got a 97% of his final exam and an A in his class. As a matter of fact, after the final exam, he emailed me: "Outstanding job, Ron. Way to go. Go, Pack, Go." He knew—and so did everyone else in the class—I am a big Green Bay Packers Fan. I remember thinking, "Wow, what a really nice guy." I remember smiling as I read his email. I even forwarded the email to Eric in a weird, uncanny twist of events. Was the professor running a Machiavellian rouge on me? Maybe he knew that, if he pissed me off, I would either sink or swim. He did come across as a curmudgeon of an old, wise owl. Guess I will never know. I hate to ask him and spoil the romanticism of it all.

My story has many morals. The explanations of my initial failure are numerous: focus, determination, apathy, and agency. Sad part is, these were things I had preached but not practiced in this specific case. I got cocky.

In the case of leadership, the lack of focus and determination will be a problem. Let me be clear: I am not talking about how fast you "like" a social media picture or re-share a video or funny text. Not that type of focus and determination. Seriously though, when you are not focused and determined, you are not connected, in-tuned and motivated on the important needs. You are stripping and disarming yourself of reaching your maximum potential and full capacity, thereby making more difficult the achievement of those personal, employment, athletic, and, in my case, academic goals.

Does that make sense?

Your objective is to stay disciplined. Stay focused on your goals and make sacrifices no matter how tough. Examine famous self-disciplined athletes, such as Serena Williams, Michael Jordan, Joe Montana, Wayne Gretzky, or Jim Brown, to name just a few. What do you see? You will see celebrated focus and determination.

Here's a counterfactual.

And here's a fact no ever wants to hear: In terms of achievement, most of what we are *not* is caused by apathy. Yes, please, familiarized yourself with said term. Apathy can be a mental speed bump, detour, or dead end. Apathy keeps many of us, including me, from progressing. I'm honest. We're friends. It is easy to embrace apathy as a virtue. Why? It is easier to take drugs than to deal with reality. It is easier to steal than to work hard for something. It is the easy wrong versus the perceived hard right. You know times when you have been apathetic but should not have been. You know it. You know others too who fit the profile. And, in some instances, it maybe be okay; however, in those things that are important to you, apathy is not okay. But who am I? Some of our world's greatest minds have not missed the dire ramifications of apathy. Einstein once said, "The world will not be destroyed by those who do evil, but by those who watch them without doing anything."

I won't let you stand by and not do anything. Because success is about doing, not dreaming. Doers are people like Nelson Mandela and Rollie Free. One fulfilled a dream of breaking through 27 years of incarceration and apartheid-ridden South Africa; the other wanted the American motorcycle land speed record so bad in the 1940s that he practically rode naked. Therefore, with your clothes on, you must have agency and motivation. Motivate yourself every day. I had a great mentor who said to me, "The hardest part of your day will be getting up every morning." You know what? He was right. I motivate myself every day to "do what I have to do, so I can do what I want to do." Sometimes, for me, it's as simple as getting out of bed. Other times, it meant working two jobs or shoveling horse manure. At the end of the day, you have to be the fire to your own engine, because nobody else will be.

All told, the hardest obstacle is managing that thing between your ears.

During my last four-plus years of Naval service, I was a High-Risk Water Survival instructor. Students all of all shapes and sizes and backgrounds entered through our doors. One of my more memorable students was built like an NFL Linebacker–6'3"and 230 lbs.; he was a rock in the water and couldn't swim to save his life. What's worse, he was terrified of water. What's worse, worse, the swimming qualification was mandatory for the linebacker's job and advancement. I had a week to get him trained, so to speak.

On that Monday morning, I asked him, "Do you know what muscle memory is?" He did not. After giving him Webster's definition of muscle memory– "the ability to repeat a specific muscular movement with improved efficiency and accuracy that is acquired through practice and repetition"–we began.

It was the first step toward gaining his trust. The rest is history, as they say. He struggled each morning, afternoon, and day, but he worked nonstop. I made him repeat the required techniques until his muscles committed the movements to memory. I slowly watched him perfect his form more and more each time. Slowly but surely, a new sense of confidence overcame him. By Thursday, a smile sprinkled with validation finally cracked his face. Pain, anger, and fear were no more. Friday, our testing day, he passed with flying colors. His fellow classmates clapped loudly, cheered, and pulled him out of the water with excitement. His pain had become our pain. Words can't begin to describe the hug he gave me. Even today, as I type, I still see the smile on his face. Interesting side note: He subsequently sent me an email explaining his plans to try out for the Navy Seals. One day he can barely swim, and the next he wants to be a part of the world's most powerful fighting force. I felt like a proud father.

Let Mr. Linebacker's story be a valuable lesson, if nothing else. If you remember nothing else, remember this: You got skills! You got skills to accomplish not only life but all your leadership goals. I have spoken and interacted with many of you. You are doing amazing things. You're engineering things. You have spirited philosophies. You're building models. And you have fascinating ideas.

Please. Unlike me initially in that college math class, unlike me forgetting muscle memory, promise a few things: Promise to be honest. Promise to be focused. Promise to be motivated. Promise to act. Being a leader depends on it.

What'd he say?

Many times over, I have been labeled an inspiring influencer. On balance, however, I prefer not writing or speaking specifically about communication. Indeed, arguably, communication, or effective communication, is the most important leadership quality. I am of the philosophy that you can lecture effective communication. But you can't teach effective communication.

In this final section, I will assign homework assignments. Your first assignment is to go back and analyze and deduce examples of effective communication throughout this book. I intentionally provided practical, passionate, and fruit-bearing examples of how effective communication shaped outcomes and outputs and me as a leader. Perhaps you will highlight these areas. Perhaps you will highlight the respecting of differences. Perhaps you will highlight areas of rapport and diplomacy. Perhaps you will highlight sections that avoid bad emotions while simultaneously curating relationships. Perhaps you will highlight sections detailing vision. Perhaps you will highlight areas detailing logical thought; the end-goal in mind is to always circle back to the objective. Perhaps you will highlight where I communicated not just the problem but potential solutions. Perhaps you will highlight the importance of storytelling. Perhaps you will highlight storytelling as "being told through a certain prism." Perhaps, from the Navy Seamen, you will highlight "we talk" when explaining recognition and how a task got completed. Perhaps you will highlight where a new swimmer learned that words have capacity. Finally, perhaps you will highlight what collaboration, ambiguity, and missing information have in common. Because you can't hear if you are not listening.

What do you mean, Ron? Life experiences have been the *most* effective tool in my effective communication tool bag. Herein, it's good to know thyself. Do you know thyself? Does guilty have a face? Please see your last effective communication homework assignment. Your assignment details and case study are below.

Social Media

Friend me. Sure, but did you know that about 40% of White Americans and about 25% of non-White Americans are surrounded exclusively by friends of their own race, according to an ongoing Reuters poll.

Shocked? I wasn't. Let's play a game. You like games, right? Look at your social media feeds. Look at the people you follow and those who follow you. Now exclude all ultra-famous and celebs. Done? Good. Now exclude all businesses and spam. Done? Good. Now look at your list of people. What do you see? If it's not clear to you, I'll tell you what you see. Does everyone remaining on those lists look like you? Tell me. Am I right? Guilty? If you aren't, you probably know several people who are.

This assignment highlights the many steps necessary to facilitate effective communication because, as George Bernard Shaw said, "The single biggest problem in communication is the illusion that it has taken place."

Freedom and fear are remarkable bedfellows. Oftentimes, in denying himself sanity, all he could do was vomit his problems. Finding a sense of détente proved impossible. Through everything he realized, he didn't know what he didn't know, an endless treasure around every experience.

Be more. Leadership with its backward and elitist definitions engulfed him like being out in the world on his own. Peace came from staring at the clear, night sky; countless stars made him reimagine how infant with the universe he was. Echoes waned. Peace with his thoughts entered.

He obtained unison. He finally realized life's innermost secret: Adversity is the achiever. Ending the nightmares by way of reality, he saw a mentor, a familiar face, a G.O.A.T. Failure was no more. There was no mystery of his graduation as the familiar face said, "I'd work for you any day."

The End

SOME QUOTES I LIKE. MOST ARE MINE.

"People who are served well by their leaders will serve others well."

"Poor leaders want you to submit to them and take your place in defeat. Great leaders want you to win and take their job someday."

"Great leaders understand the continuity of leadership."

"People who cling to power tend to be poor listeners."

"Leadership: Sometimes you must suffer fools."

"Leadership is like being a real estate developer. Where others see nothing, or nothing in others, you must see a community, or an heir."

"Slow to judge. Quick to listen. Eager to learn."

"Don't let the only change you accept be the change that benefits you."

"A leader must remember leadership is a revolution

in training."

"Fix the problem, and not the blame."

"Age is not synonymous with wisdom; you can be a leader at any age."

"A leader's greatest ability will be her ability to learn and unlearn."

"Don't forget: Everyone has an agenda–including you."

"If you have a primal need to tell people what to do…leadership is not for you."

"One minute you can be the hero. The next you can be the bum; they'll ask you if you want the window or the aisle."

"One of the most important questions you can ask as a leader is: What can I do to help?"

"People love consistency; it's a human thing. Poor leaders are Dr. Jekyll and Mr. Hyde. One day they're incredulously happy. One day they're remotely Snuffleupagas sad. One day they're unconscionably irritable. It's okay to have moods. It's not so much okay to be moody."

"There's beauty in simplicity."

"Time is our most precious resource we possess."

"Our reputation is the sum of our consequential decisions."

*I could always understand the inspiring spirit,
rather than the political brain.*

To: Mayor Kevin Johnson
From: Ron Holloway
Date: 3/1/2011
Subject: A Student in Need of Help

Hello Mr. Johnson,

I am a student and former Navy veteran. I am working on a research paper for my undergraduate research design course about athletes as political actors. I have followed your career closely. Moreover, I would be extremely grateful if I could receive a short comment or comments as to why you wanted to enter the political sphere. Thanks, Sir. I look forward to your reply.

Very Respectfully,
Ron Holloway
U.S. Navy veteran

To: Ron Holloway
From: Mayor Kevin Johnson
Date: 3/1/11
Subject: A Student in Need of Help

Ron,

First, thank you for your service to our country. I appreciate your question.

My grandfather always taught me that if I saw something wrong in the world, I couldn't sit on the sidelines. I had to get involved. When I saw the cycle of poverty repeating itself in my neighborhood, I started an after-school program, charter schools, and worked on economic and community development initiatives in my community. I always saw myself as an advocate for change outside the political arena until it became clear to me that Sacramento needed new leadership to become a world class city.

I realized then that I needed to work for change inside the political arena. It has been incredibly challenging, but certainly rewarding at the same time. I love Sacramento, so it is always an honor and a pleasure to help make the city a place that works for everyone.

Best,
Kevin

LEADERSHIP
KEY TERMS

Absolute Advantage – In the theory of international trade, a country or firm has an absolute advantage if it can produce a product (good or service) more "efficiently" (cheaply) than others. (critically think how this comes into place with leadership).

Actionable – Capable of being acted on.

Anchoring Biases – The act of basing a judgment on a familiar reference point that is incomplete or irrelevant to the problem that is being solved.

Behavior – The way in which someone conducts oneself; the way in which something functions or operates.

Characteristic – A distinguishing trait, quality, or property.

Cognitive Dissonance – Psychological conflict resulting from incongruous beliefs and attitudes held simultaneously. i.e. smoking a cigarette. You know it's bad for you; but you do it anyway.

Collaboration – To work jointly with others or together especially in an intellectual endeavor.

Comparative Advantage – Concept in economics that a country should specialize in producing and exporting only those goods and services which it can produce more efficiently (at lower opportunity cost) than other goods and services (which it should import).

Confirmation Bias – Suggests that we don't perceive circumstances objectively. We pick out those bits of data that make us feel good because they confirm our prejudices.

Courtesy Flush – The showing of politeness in one's attitude while detoxifying on the toilet by causing large quantities of water to pass through in order to reduce foul aroma.

Culture – The customary beliefs, social forms, and material traits of a racial, religious, or social group.

Curating – Person charged with the care of souls, parish priest; to act as curator of.

Discipline – Training that corrects, molds, or perfects the mental faculties.

Dynamic – Marked by usually continuous and productive activity or change.

Empathy – The action of understanding, being aware of, being sensitive to, and vicariously experiencing the feelings, thoughts, and experience of another of either the past or present without having the feelings, thoughts, and experience fully communicated in an objectively explicit manner.

Ethnocentrism – The attitude that one's own group, ethnicity, or nationality is superior to others.

Fallacy – A false or mistaken idea.

Followership – The capacity or willingness to follow a leader (or anyone I'd add).

Goal – The end toward which effort is directed.

Halo Effect – Our tendency to recognize one positive or negative quality or trait of a person, and then associate that quality or trait with everything about that person.

Inclusive – Broad in orientation or scope.

Insanity – "Doing the same thing over and over again and expecting different results." – Unknown

Leadership – Leadership is the art of getting someone else to do something you want done because he wants to do it. —General Dwight Eisenhower

Manager – A person who conducts business or household affairs.

Measure – The dimensions, capacity, or amount of something ascertained by measuring.

Modeling – An example for imitation or emulation.

Motivation – A motivating force, stimulus, or influence.

Myopic – Lacking in foresight or discernment: narrow in perspective and without concern for broader implications.

Nutrition – The act or process of nourishing or being nourished; specifically: the sum of the processes by which an animal or plant takes in and utilizes food substances.

Power – Possession of control, authority, or influence over others.

Specific – Free from ambiguity.

Static – Exerting force by reason of weight alone without motion.

Subconscious – Existing in the mind but not immediately available to consciousness.

Systems Thinking: Practice of thinking that takes a holistic view of complex events or phenomenon, seemingly caused by myriad of isolated, independent, and usually unpredictable factors or forces.

Teachable Moment – A time that is favorable for teaching something, such as proper behavior.

Trait – A distinguishing quality (as of personal character).

Transition – Passage from one state, stage, subject, or place to another.

Trust – Assured reliance on the character, ability, strength, or truth of someone or something.

Uncertainty Reduction Theory – If you get this, you've obtained the cheat code. Study this. Research this. Anticipate how it affects many aspects of our lives. Anticipate communication before it happens.

Value(s) – Something (such as a principle or quality) intrinsically valuable or desirable.

Vision – Mode of seeing or conceiving (2): unusual discernment or foresight - a person of vision.

"Leadership is personal not positional." -Danesia Parker—a bright, beautiful, and talented young lady whom shared this with me through her equally bright, beautiful, and talented mother.

ABOUT THE AUTHOR

Ron Holloway, a Milwaukee, WI native, resides in the Washington DC metro area where he is a motivational speaker who is changing lives and inspires others to do the same. Ron's books cost less than a latte and are part of the newest literary trend of short books, which make those with short attention spans very happy. More info can be found at iamronholloway.com.

STAY UPDATED

iamronholloway.com

Made in the USA
Las Vegas, NV
17 June 2022